A special gift for you

To

Christina

From

Nancy B

Introduction

During World War II a woman received a letter from a soldier she didn't know. His name was Murray and he wrote from the battlefield.

Murray wrote that he had once been in her Sunday school class and she had spoken about Jesus Christ as a hero for boys. He mentioned the date when this woman's words had altered his whole perspective on life.

This lady had kept a diary all of her life, so she quickly turned to the date that Murray had mentioned. She learned that she had come home from that Sunday school session very discouraged and even thought about giving up teaching.

The entry for that day read "Had an awful time. The boys were so restless. I am not cut out for this kind of thing. I had to take two classes together. No one listened, except at the end, a boy named Murray from the other class seemed to be taking it in. He grew very quiet and subdued, but I expect he was just tired of playing."

Just as the shadows of that nameless woman had fallen across that boy's life to make a lasting impression, none of us will ever know how our lives and faith and talk will influence others around us.

Mother, you have no idea how those seeds of love and caring will impact a young life! The Bible reminds us that we should not grow weary in our well-doing, because sometime down the road, "in due season," we will be reaping a harvest! No day is wasted when it is spent with your children! Don't give up. Don't be discouraged — today may impact a life forever.

'There's O N L Y O N E

PRETTY child in the world,

and every mother has it."

— *Traditional Proverb*

It is a good thing to give thanks unto the Lord, and to sing praises unto thy name, O most High: To shew forth thy lovingkindness in the morning, and thy faithfulness every night. — King David

"A baby is

GOD'S OPINION

that the **world**

SHOULD go on."

— *Carl Sandburg*

. . . He that keepeth thee will
not slumber. — King David

"People who say they

SLEEP

like a

baby

usually *DON'T
HAVE* one."

— Leo J. Burke

*As newborn babes, desire the sincere
milk of the word, that ye may grow
thereby.* — I Pet. 2:2

MOTHERHOOD:

For I was my father's son, tender and only beloved in the sight of my mother. — Prov. 4:3

ALL LOVE

begins and

ends there."

— *Robert Browning*

"There was *NEVER* a child so *lovely*

but his MOTHER
was *GLAD* to get
him to
sleep."

— Ralph Waldo Emerson

I will both lay me down in peace, and sleep: for thou, LORD, only makest me dwell in safety. — Ps. 4:8

"A baby is an *angel*

whose

WINGS

decrease

as his

LEGS

increase."

The angel of the LORD encampeth round about them that fear him, and delivereth them. — Ps. 34:7

— *Unknown*

"There is **N O** influence

so *POWERFUL*

as that of the *mother.*"

— *Sarah Josepha Hale*

... for the joy of the LORD is your strength. — Neh. 8:10

"GOD

could not be *everywhere*

He that dwelleth in the secret place of the most High shall abide under the shadow of the Almighty. I will say of the LORD, He is my refuge and my fortress: my God; in him will I trust. — Ps. 91:1,2

and

therefore

He made

ᴍᴏᴛʜᴇʀs."

— *Jewish Proverb*

"LAWYERS, I SUPPOSE,

*Therefore, my beloved brethren, be ye stedfast, unmoveable,
always abounding in the work of the Lord, forasmuch as ye know
that your labour is not in vain in the Lord.* — 1 Cor. 15:58

were

children

ONCE."

— *Charles Lamb*

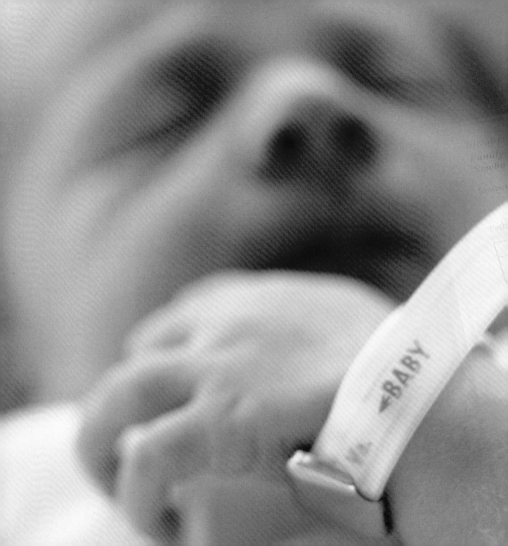

"Babies are such a *NICE* way

to *START*

people."

— Don Herrold

Before I formed thee in the belly I knew thee; and before thou camest forth out of the womb I sanctified thee, and I ordained thee a prophet unto the nations. — Jer. 1:5

"A *baby* will make . . .

LOVE **STRONGER,**

days **shorter,** nights

l o n g e r, bankroll

smaller, home HAPPIER,

clothes shabbier, the past

forgotten, and the future

worth living for."

— Unknown

Ponder the path of thy feet, and let all thy
ways be established. — Prov. 4:26

"SWEET BABE,
in thy *face*

Soft desires I can trace,
Secret joys and secret smiles,
Little pretty infant wiles. "

— *William Blake*

Shew me thy ways, O LORD; teach me thy paths. Lead me in thy truth, and teach me: for thou art the God of my salvation; on thee do I wait all the day. — Ps. 25:4,5

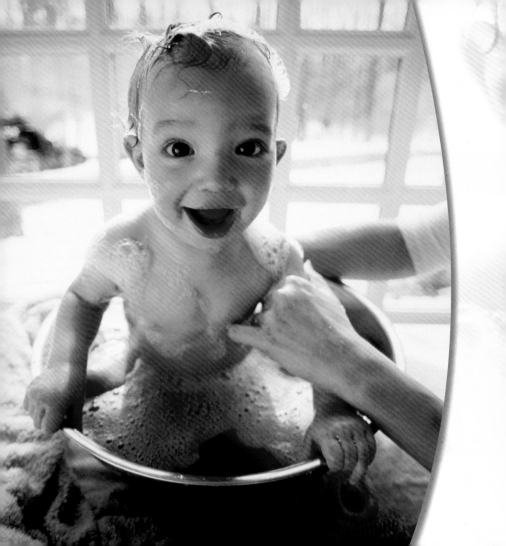

"If evolution

REALLY works,

how come mothers

only have

TWO hands?"

— Milton Berle

I will praise thee; for I am fearfully
and wonderfully made: marvellous
are thy works; and that my soul
knoweth right well. — Ps. 139:14

"Raising KIDS

Train up a child in the way he should go: and when he is old, he will not depart from it. — Prov. 22:6

is part JOY

and part

GUERILLA WARFARE."

— *Ed Asner*

"CHILDREN are the hands

I will teach you by the hand of God: that which is
with the Almighty will I not conceal. — Job 27:11

by which we

TAKE HOLD

of *heaven*."

— Henry Ward Beecher

" **Y**ou can *LEARN* many things from children.

A merry heart doeth good like a medicine.... — Prov. 17:22

How Much

PATIENCE

you have, for

instance."

— *Franklin P. Jones*

"**T**here is a garden in *EVERY CHILDHOOD*, an *enchanted place* where colors are B R I G H T E R, the air S O F T E R, and the morning *more fragrant* than ever again."

— *Elizabeth Lawrence*

And thine age shall be clearer than the noonday; thou shalt shine forth, thou shalt be as the morning. — Job 11:17

" *Far away* in the *universe*

ARE MY HIGHEST ASPIRATIONS.

I may not reach them, but I can **LOOK UP**
and see their beauty, **BELIEVE IN** them, and
try to *follow* where they lead."

— *Louisa May Alcott*

When I consider thy heavens, the work of thy fingers,
the moon and the stars, which thou hast ordained;
What is man, that thou art mindful of him? and the
son of man, that thou visitest him? — Ps. 8:3,4

"The great HIGH of winning

WIMBLEDON

lasts for about a
WEEK.

You go down in the record book, but you don't have anything *TANGIBLE* to hold on to.

But having a BABY —

there isn't **ANY** comparison."

— *Chris Evert Lloyd*

Because he hath set his love upon me, therefore will I deliver him: I will set him on high, because he hath known my name. — Ps. 91:14

"*I HATE IT*

when my foot

FALLS ASLEEP

during the day

'cause that means

it's going to be

UP ALL NIGHT."

— *Stephen Wright*

"A *mother*

NEVER
REALIZES
that her children are
no longer children."

— Don Herrold